Hello, America!

# Ellis Island

by R.J. Bailey

NATIONAL PARK SERVICE

Department of the Interior

## Ellis Island
## Immigration Museum
### Statue of Liberty National Monument

National Park Service
United States Department of the Interior

Bullfrog Books

# Ideas for Parents and Teachers

Bullfrog Books let children practice reading informational text at the earliest reading levels. Repetition, familiar words, and photo labels support early readers.

## Before Reading
• Discuss the cover photo. What does it tell them?

• Look at the picture glossary together. Read and discuss the words.

## Read the Book
• "Walk" through the book and look at the photos. Let the child ask questions. Point out the photo labels.

• Read the book to the child, or have him or her read independently.

## After Reading
• Prompt the child to think more. Ask: Have you ever been to Ellis Island? Did your ancestors travel through Ellis Island?

Bullfrog Books are published by Jump!
5357 Penn Avenue South
Minneapolis, MN 55419
www.jumplibrary.com

Library of Congress Cataloging-in-Publication Data

Names: Bailey, R.J., author.
Title: Ellis Island / by R.J. Bailey.
Description: Minneapolis, MN: Jump!, Inc., [2017].
Series: Hello, America! | Includes index.
Identifiers: LCCN 2016008980 (print)
LCCN 2016010139 (ebook)
ISBN 9781620313480 (hard cover: alk. paper)
ISBN 9781624963957 (e-book)
Subjects: LCSH: Ellis Island Immigration Station (N.Y. and N.J.)—Juvenile literature.
Ellis Island (N.J. and N.Y.)—History—Juvenile literature. United States—Emigration and immigration—Juvenile literature.
Classification: LCC JV6484 .B35 2017 (print)
LCC JV6484 (ebook) | DDC 304.8/73—dc23
LC record available at http://lccn.loc.gov/2016008980

Editor: Kirsten Chang
Series Designer: Ellen Huber
Book Designer: Molly Ballanger
Photo Researcher: Kirsten Chang

Photo Credits: All photos by Shutterstock except: Alamy, 6–7, 12–13, 18–19, 22bl, 23tl; Corbis, 14–15; Getty, 16, 22tr, 22br; Gjenvick-Gjønvik Archives, 17; iStock, 24; Sean Pavone/Shutterstock.com, 13; Superstock, 20–21; Thinkstock, 1, 3, 4, 23ml.

Printed in the United States of America at Corporate Graphics in North Mankato, Minnesota.

# Table of Contents

# Island of Hope

Get off the boat.

We are here!

**Where? Ellis Island.**

**It is in New York Harbor.**

immigrants

Long ago, people in Europe
wanted a new life.

They left their homes.

Where did they go?
America!

We call them
immigrants.

They got on ships.
They crossed
the ocean.

Look! The Statue of Liberty.

Immigrants saw it, too.

They were happy.

They were in America!
Their first stop was
Ellis Island.

Great
Hall

We go to a big room.

People waited here.

They put down
their bags.

Doctors looked at them.

Were they healthy?

Were they sick?

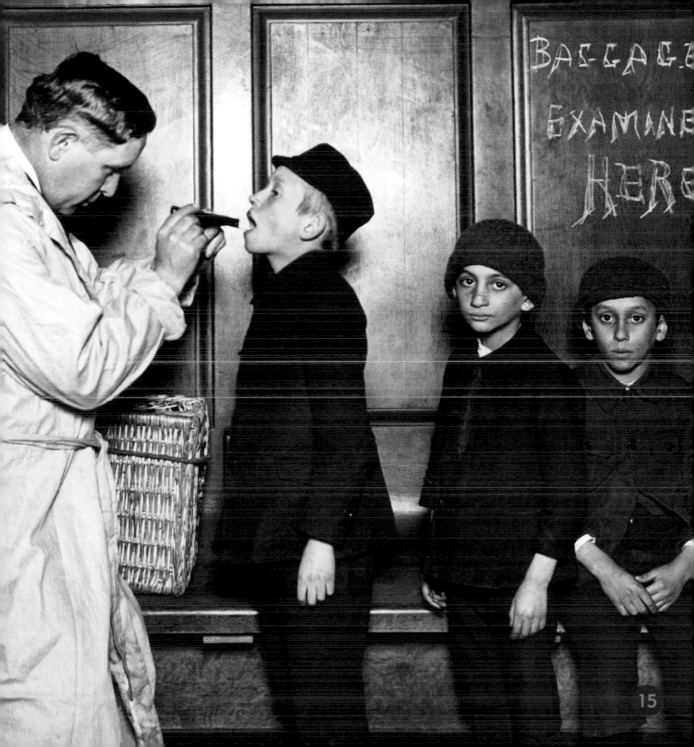
15

**They had papers.**

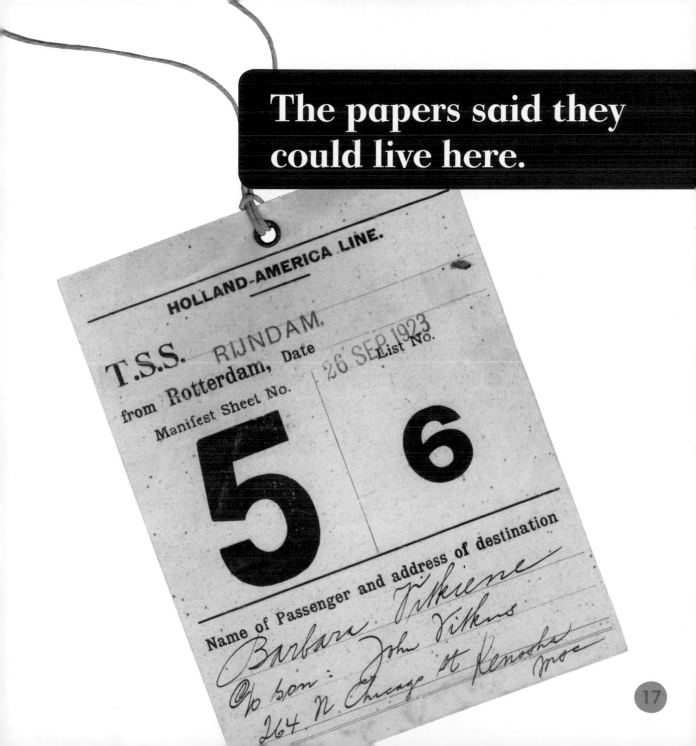

The papers said they could live here.

HOLLAND-AMERICA LINE.

T.S.S. RIJNDAM.
from Rotterdam, Date    26 SEP 1923    List No.

Manifest Sheet No.

5          6

Name of Passenger and address of destination

Barbara Vikiene
C/o son: John Vikus
264 N. Chicago St Kenosha
Wisc

They gave their names.
Look! We read their
names on a big wall.
They are our
ancestors.

# America is our home!

# A Day at Ellis Island

Statue of Liberty

Immigration Museum

Great Hall

Wall of Honor

# Picture Glossary

**ancestors**
Members of a family who lived a long time ago.

**immigrants**
People from one country who move to another country to live.

**Europe**
A continent that is north of Africa and between Asia and the Atlantic Ocean.

**island**
Land that is circled by water.

**harbor**
A place on the coast where boats and ships can enter.

**New York**
The largest city in New York state.

23

# Index

# To Learn More

Learning more is as easy as 1, 2, 3.

1) Go to www.factsurfer.com

2) Enter "EllisIsland" into the search box.

3) Click the "Surf" button to see a list of websites.

With factsurfer.com, finding more information is just a click away.